Boyd and Floyd Join the Dig

By Eliza Webb

Boyd and Floyd sat on the couch and enjoyed a game.

"Cowboy Roy is a great game!" Floyd yelled.

"I'm the best at this game!" Boyd said.

Mum needed a ploy
to get the boys outside.

Mum's friend Beth would come
to the house.

Beth spoiled Boyd and Floyd!

"My job is to dig in soil for old things like pots and tools," Beth said.

"Join me!"

The next day, Boyd and Floyd joined Beth.

They dug in moist, brown topsoil with small spades.

Boyd and Floyd toiled.

They dug up bits of old pots.

“Those pots would have been good for boiling stew,” Beth said.

Boyd pointed at an object
in the soil.
He dug it out.

“It’s a coin!” Floyd called.

The coin had a coiled snake on it.

Boys, this coin is very old!

At home, Floyd said,
"Let's sell the coin
and get a Cowboy Roy toy!"

"Don't sell it," Beth said.
"Give it to a museum,
so people can enjoy it!"

That's a great point, Beth.

CHECKING FOR MEANING

1. What was Mum's ploy to get the boys out of the house? *(Literal)*
2. What was on the coin that the boys found? *(Literal)*
3. Did the boys like Beth? How do you know? *(Inferential)*

EXTENDING VOCABULARY

cowboy	What are the two smaller words in the word *cowboy*? How do these two smaller words help you understand the meaning of *cowboy*? What jobs do cowboys do on a ranch or farm?
ploy	Read the sentence *Mum needed a ploy to get the boys outside*. What do you think a ploy is? What is another word the author could have used instead of *ploy*?
toiled	What is the base of the word *toiled*? What does it mean to toil? What is another word the author could have used?

MOVING BEYOND THE TEXT

1. Archaeologists like Beth work at special dig sites to try to find interesting things from the past. These things were left behind by humans who lived many years ago. What kinds of things might archaeologists dig up?
2. What are some outdoor activities that you enjoy?
3. What other types of objects are found in museums? Have you ever been to a museum?
4. Beth and the boys wore hats, vests and gloves at the dig site. Why is this gear important? They used spades to dig. What other tools or equipment might they have used at the dig site?

TIME TO WRITE

Write the next part of this story. Describe what might have happened after Boyd and Floyd gave the coin to a museum.

PRACTICE WORDS